Moles

Curious Kids Press

Please note:All Rights Reserved. No part of this publication may be reproduced in any form or by any means, including scanning, photocopying, or otherwise without prior written permission of the copyright holder. Copyright © 2014

Moles

There is 20 different species of the Mole. This animal is not a rodent. It belongs in the family of Insectivores and is closely related to the Shrew. The Mole is an odd looking animal, which you will discover in greater detail later on. In fact, in this book we are going to discover all sorts of cool facts about the Mole, like where it can be found, its extraordinary abilities and much more. Read on to be totally amazed with this strange creature.

Where in the World?

Did you know there are no moles found in Ireland? Moles are found in Europe, Asia, South Africa and North America. They live under the ground. Some species of moles are also aquatic or semi-aquatic. This means they like to spend time in the water.

The Body of a Mole

Did you know moles are quite small? The body of a mole is cylindrical in shape. Depending on the species, it can measure from 4.7 to 5.9 inches long (12 to 15 centimeters). It does not have a neck, but it does have a pointed nose, stout forearms and is covered in thick, dark fur.

The Mole's Senses

Did you know moles are not blind? However, they do have very poor eyesight. Their eyes and ears are very small and usually covered in fur. The most powerful sense the mole has is its sense of smell. It has an area of bare pink skin on the snout. It is covered in tiny pimples that detect movement. It can also detect the scents of prey and other moles.

The Feet of a Mole

Did you know Moles have broad front feet? Most moles have big feet for their overall size. Their paws each have stout claws that face outward. These are specially designed for digging. Moles are fast diggers and can tunnel at a rate of 15 feet-per-hour (4.5 meters-per-hour). Shallow tunnels can be built at a rate of 12 inches-per-minute (30.4 centimeters-per-minute)..

Mole Tunnels

Did you know the mole will build two types of tunnels? These can be surface tunnels and deep tunnels. Surface tunnels are located 1 to 4 inches (2.54 to 10 centimeters) below the surface. These surface tunnels connect with deeper runways that are located 3 to 12 inches (7.6 to 30 centimeters). It can be as deep as 40 inches (101.6 centimeters)..

What a Mole Eats

Did you know Moles are omnivores? This means they will eat most anything, but they do prefer earthworms. Larger moles have been known to catch and eat mice. The mole also has a special saliva in its mouth. This contains a toxin that can paralyze small animals and earthworms.

The Mole's Special Ability

Did you know the mole can breath deep under the ground? This is because moles can tolerate higher levels of carbon dioxide than other mammals. They can also reuse the oxygen they inhale when they are above ground. All this gives the mole the ability to stay for long periods of time underground.

Mole Mom

Did you know the Moles breed between March and May? The female mole will carry her young for 30 days. She can have 1 to 2 litters each year. Each litter has 3 to 6 babies, which mom mole will suckle for about 5 weeks.

The Baby Moles

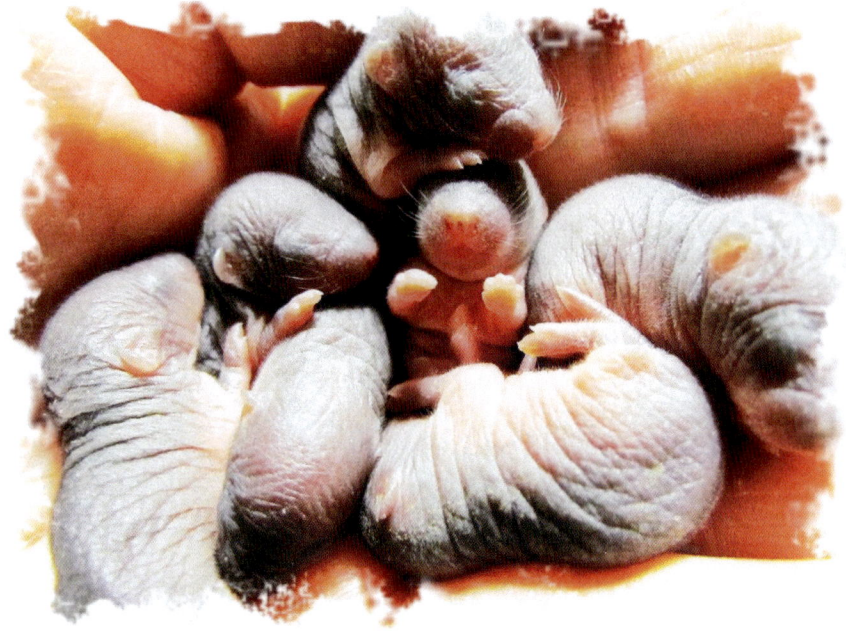

Did you know baby moles are called, pups? The baby moles are born very tiny. They are nearly hairless and cannot see or hear. These pups are completely dependant on the mom mole. After about a month the baby moles will be able to be on their own.

Predators of the Mole

Did you know this animal has many natural predators? Due to their small size, moles are preyed on by mammals, birds and reptiles. Moles underground have less chance to be preyed upon. However, when they are in their burrows they are more likely to be dug up by gardeners with their spades.

The Mole and People

Did you know people consider moles to be pests? Because these animals are able to dig deep and long tunnels, many people find them to be a pest. As we learned earlier, moles can dig very quickly. This can ruin people's lawns and also gardens. Moles on a golf course can create quite a mess.

Life of a Mole

Did you know the average lifespan of a mole is about 4 years-old? However, some species of mole have been known to live until they are 6 or 7 years-old. It may be difficult to spot a mole since it spends most of its time under the ground.

The Star-nosed Mole

Did you know this mole has a star-shaped end on its snout? This super-star-snout can detect food very quickly. In fact, this mole can catch and eat food faster than we can see it. It has 11 spongy, finger-like appendages on the end of its snout that helps it do this.

Eastern Mole

Did you know this mole is medium-size with large, hairless and spade-shaped forefeet? Its large feet are perfect for digging. It is a common mole found in North America. It prefers to live in the woods, fields, pastures, and meadows. It will build both deep and shallow burrows.

Shrew

Did you know the shrew is closely related to the mole? Shrews can be found in most areas of the world. They have sharp, spike-like teeth. They like to eat seeds, insects, nuts, worms and a variety of other foods. Some can climb trees, live underground, live under snow or even hunt in water.

Quiz

Question 1: How many species of moles are there?

Answer 1: 20 different species

Question 2: What are the 2 types of tunnels a mole will dig?

Answer 2: Surface tunnels and deep tunnels

Question 3: What is the mole's special ability?

Answer 3: It can breath underground

Question 4: What are baby moles called?

Answer 4: Pups

Question 5: What do people consider moles to be?

Answer 5: Pests

Thank you for checking out another title from Curious Kids Press! Make sure to search "Curious Kids Press" on Amazon.com for many other great books.

Printed in Poland
by Amazon Fulfillment
Poland Sp. z o.o., Wrocław